**DARK LETTER DAYS**
Collected Works

By

Lorin Morgan-Richards

author of
"A Dredged Summons," Etc.
A Raven Above Press
Studio City, CA
www.aravenabovepress.com

Paperback © 2016

ALL RIGHTS RESERVED

DEDICATED TO KAREN

All the Characters and Events portrayed in this book are the creation of Lorin Morgan-Richards

A RAVEN ABOVE PRESS PUBLICATION

ISBN 978-0-9973193-0-9

# Index

| | |
|---|---|
| 1. Someone Else's Mug | 5 |
| 2. Love and Blue | 7 |
| 3. Crabs of Coronado | 9 |
| 4. Celestial Son | 11 |
| 5. The isle of youth dramatic | 13 |
| 6. Praise, Praise the Jazzing Damned | 15 |
| 7. What good have I endured? | 17 |
| 8. The Roundabout | 21 |
| 9. Blue Run | 23 |
| 10. That Black Book | 25 |
| 11. I'm a lowly woodcutter | 27 |
| 12. Fragile Hands | 29 |
| 13. Alone | 31 |
| 14. The Casual Voyeur of the Soul | 33 |
| 15. Impatience and the burned out mind | 35 |
| 16. The Boiling Shrimp | 37 |
| 17. Shadows Allure | 39 |
| 18. Chelsea Hotel: Vandalism and other changes removed | 41 |
| 19. Jumping the Curb | 43 |
| 20. Comforting a Dying Mantis | 45 |
| 21. Buzz and Flutter | 47 |
| 22. The Persistent Fly | 49 |
| 23. Pendulum | 51 |

## Someone Else's Mug

Four metal chairs snug gently under the shelf of an empty mug.

A light hits their frame at a bend,
shadowing existence and illuminating the floor underneath.

The alien sky is in our water
an abducted sea monster
a face to reconnect us.

There in the stars
a line is forming,
they call this place the commissaire.

People are here to stay,
people are here to nest.

Abound in my thoughts I listen.
I do not wish to bring up petty grievances
but I would just as easily disconnect from the world one should not hear.

What is the point of relaying every word when the words become the crime of friendship.

I do not find myself moving further.
and I consume more vats of temporary cures in the cursing back of the cafe.

I try to wake myself from this sandstorm.
Is it the suffering of my craft that produces this paralysis?

What say do I have of the minstrels cloak?

Am i the ugly one?

The transcendental peering in the shadows for reflection.

And i feel engulfed when it runs dry.

The imagination of words weaken the expression as a thousand wrinkles of fine lines state the fallacy that is otherwise speechless.

The chairs are now full and each traveler down their eyes afixed to their vice.

Two of the four mingle
redistributing the shadows
leaving only a small box of light.

Though the fool is said to follie
it is for their own protection.

And i begin to doubt myself again.

## **Love and Blue**

Love and blue
Love and blue

Blackbird in the sky
Hold me up
Tell me why
I struggle
I struggle.

Where is my nest?
Here
Or there
anywhere?

You must look into the past to see your self
Is it what you've always wanted?

Blackbird in the sky
Hold me up
Tell me why
I struggle
I struggle.

You
And
Me.

Love and blue
Love and blue.

## Crabs of Coronado

Crabs of Coronado
awash in your excess.
Displace the messenger
Extraneous matters herein.

Chase the seagulls
fly with the pigeons tails.
Lucky tall hats atop
the Strawberry haired twins.

Trip and skin,
the seeping clouds soften.
Dressed in seaweed coats
and abalone sin.

I found the clues,
Scattered ashore
with weather whirling
the summer carousel spins.

Love stranger,
Ease the signal.
Pipes adore,
You never know what the waves will bring in.

I change my vantage,
Back up!
Secretly possessed,
scavenging my ticket
to the palace of Gwynn.

# Celestial Son

The universe is made of our thoughts.
Our thoughts are infinite.

Creation is provided in our being
inside the womb and before,
each stage presents itself in the child.
What we were and what we have become.
We rose from water,
introduced in a spectacle of conception.
Our DNA adapts
to what we know now as life.
Gravity is our evolution,
longer, shorter
we evolve to live
in the period of time before us.

Pyramids laugh at the mystic fire,
Seasons breath unrest.

Two elementals.
Earth and song.
The celestial choir finds survival.
Death consumes.
While one or a few,
cleared the atmosphere
to attach to the Earth's lining,
The early mineral form.

An anomalous donor in space
spreading its seed from a pulsating Star.

# The isle of youth dramatic

The isle of youth dramatic,
classifies the systematic convention.
Ordered and enabled
by a chaotic disease detoxifying.
Hanging from a rutter
complicating the web.
As the linear notes leak,
constraint.
And make the ideal proportion,
out of nothing.
Falling further behind the times.
Farther and sharply
feral of the truth.
No end point.
No result given.
Giving 199 percent.
Powered and cursed
an anti-social socialite.
Playground dreams
A nameless bully
on his bike and the girl.
Facelessly absorbed
around them.
A death threat
A cache of taunts.
Revealing his own recklessness.
Let him pass. Let him pass.
Slow, and take a step.
Undefeated.
Do not limit yourself to what people say.
Fly beyond the borders of illusion and comfort.

## Praise, Praise the Jazzing Damned

Praise, praise to the jazzing damned
Who glean and silt
off the stagnating stratosphere.
The mother of pearl
brace and cling
to the bosom
Of her old rusty chariot.

A once golden chalice
unfolded
bobbing and wobbling
in the Irish sea.

She responds to nature with a gentle kiss
a clipped fairy wing,
placed delicately in the virgin tree.

Her naked legs
bound and lock
announcing
the changing
of the season.

Amending each day
Sleeping
Praying
of her mantis pharaoh.

She breaks free
Of heavens molt
Crawling outside her
cascading casket.

Gasping for life
dressed and appeased
to the painful haunt
that brings her life out of her shell.

A stone offer
rejected
the jeckyling
Hyde
who draw prisms
through her glades
of golden nectar.

To the punished poet
who dances
wildly
burgeoning and budding
to find his neverending home.

A swinging aster
swaying
the direction of the stars
weighing,
in thought
his heart wailing.

The loss
shriveled and mistaken
shedding his brow
taking the road underground.

Discovering
the world of worms
pretending
Its everything he found.

## What good have I endured?

I have seen these salty seas
over rugged shipwrecked falls,
of walking the planked ford
with pockets of luck and despair.

I have drawn lines invisible
and nested deeds not owed but worn.
I've rang bells of five lots to those
seen waving and smiling ever' forth.

What good have I become?

Turrets of rum cry from my battered eyes,
as my weathered pupils blast a beaming Driscoll dance.

My feet twist up
and I notice myself slipping back.
Avoiding your delivered stance.

Never call the wintry howl.

Harboring ships to sea
A new life begins
Setting the course for you and me.

The village weeps under the flag
And the protruding red light
Of the ocean plight
deflects my inner ear.

I gravitate to the cave of sorrow
With a treasure map in hand
I squeezed the water out

and dry off the half red sand.

What good am I ashore?

Chances swing by the pale palm moonlight,
hanging on a glider weight
as long as I see the red sky at night.

What good am I?

Sitting on a juvenile seat,
primrose and ivy
charades and appliquéd
fortune is not for the meek.

But the stabled gold aplenty
all for me to allure.
What is at loss is just a penny...

What good have I endured?

# The Roundabout

The bar goes on the other way
I made the same mistake.
No reply contends the air
She seizes the point.

Spinning, holding you out
The roundabout sing
Sidewalks at your feet.

Is there another life
through a roadway split?

Running away
finding bullets
pretending they are lipstick.

You learn more about yourself
When you do not pretend to be yourself.

At the table we meet
disagreeable in resolution
your rain welcomes the slums of my heart.

But your horrible crickets and ants
will eventually carry me away
with pitiful destruction.

## Blue Run

A nesting bird is a lighthouse to the soul,
a nights watchman for the hunter's return.

The vestige of soiled fingers crack the divining rod as
pregnant blossoms dance the joyous roots.

A broken toy thrown into the canvas is cherished is by
another.

Rays of the sun on water are reflective.
Projections of the sun on a rock is blinding.
If I am to return with the seed that feeds,
I must hurry back to the fields before me.

A caveated water slide,
a monsterous gate.
Nestled plants seclude
the papal rings that meditate.
Walking up a hill's parade
to see your grave
and the trash
of two bony dogs
discarded and laid.

When all our wings mounted
gawking at four corners
questioning
When did we forget?
What have we lost?
What have we won?
What have we become?

# That Black Book

Footsteps order the past
erased by the afforded who track our existence.

Brunettes come to the store
the blue eye adore
how drawn their ways
speaking to themselves like a grinning child.

When I was conceived I was grieved.
Sharing a common fate by material hands
repeated infinitely by those that brush against it.

We ask of you
but you repent.
Sucking the magic out of life
going to patty-pat-pat,
on the backs of your rank and file
until reverence bespeaks you.

Oh grizzly cross
what do I owe of thee?
You know nothing of the ill willed
distempered and reason there,
the pegged arm chair,
of disgrace and disappointment
for the common man.

And you go down to take your own.

Missionaries perfumed the land
shrouded in a torquoise veil
with vile means
dropping skeptics under glass
Imposter I say, Imposter!
Is there nothing true?
Nothing possible?
A fable.

That black covered book,
Is it raining where you are?

## I'm a Lowly Woodcutter

The roadside burns with violent weeds
cutting my face.
Open the shades
let your dreams in
see it
remain.

Focus.
I cannot be like you.
I am not you.
My path is my own.

I will not cut the wood,
but I will do my share
and sit beside the roots.

Today I'm in charge,
drowning out the croaking.
I'll pitch my tent,
and echo off the prison chamber
at all hours, all day baby.

Carved out in desecrated sap
A lovers name
A broken hand rail
I'm a lowly woodcutter.

Catering and cantering,
a stranger remarks
"at the end of the day."
you are gone
so fleetless
So free.

## Fragile Hands

I was leaning on fragile hands most pleasing,
Protecting the ragged weed.

My arms green and shaking,
bending towards a dry follicle bed.

Your dirty pup attacked my gracious ascent,
lifting above a three ring climb.

An arrow pointing line
with finely paneled windows.
Scribbling in and out
counting 3, then in opposite
until the walls fell.
And I turned to the whimpering feet of the clouds
her wet hair dropping ginger from the hills.
Counting brilliance,
I suggested on rice as I knew no other.

As she said with a raised brow,
"We live in gardens, communal, and fenced."
Rotted at the root, So pretty outside.
Planted freely, cherry planters shiny and shoes.
Stretched into neighboring fields,
but attached to pests and weeds.
Water feeds us.
Water doesn't need us.

We are intertwined with those around us,
a circus of an interwoven song.
Has our luck nearly vanished?

## Alone

Alone,
There is a world of thoughts streaming,
uninhibited and romanticized.
There is a voice that stiffens through the numbness,
A beautiful, unbeaten, strong voice.
Which does not rely on conventions of melody,
But still places every note in an ideal way.

There needs no extra words to be spoken.
Power is breath.
Power is patience.
Power is something more to concentrate.

How timeless it is to be,
to have breath and no willingness to be heard.
But to have those words
buzz gently
Or riff smoothly to the self.

A strong voice,
Alone.
With your words,
And my thoughts.

No long for more.

# The Casual Voyeur of the Soul

The solar body aligns
with cosmic organs swallow in digestion.

A superlative star,
Pluto acts in the third scene
as a frigid spleen transplanted.

That stench,
that horrible stench holding corpse
in the fountains of our mind.

Bells ring on a giant sail
echoing the pyschosomatic trauma
I cannot say who I am not.

We are not the same in the reflection.
Distance has aged us.
Intimate is the eye the stone breast of four flights.

Caressing the grey mirrored steps,
a circle around the sun.
Shadows behind me of idle and idleness
the world of race,
before you retire.

The deafening loss of the dark trance,
to the children of the moon
and the hunter Orion
will be obsolete to the cause.

# Impatience and the Burned Out Mind

After getting my coffee
I came to a crosswalk and waited.
I felt a presence coming up behind me.

Stinking of the sewer.
It was a half man and half monster,
with a drooping tongue,
and blistering stretch of limbs.
The elements had worn his face
and his body was twisted around
trapped atop a ceaseless merry-go-round.
His pupils had faded and a green residue poured out of the
sides of his mouth when he spoke.
But there were no words.

I glanced around him nervously and tried to make a comment
to suppress my anxiety, "poetic, deep," I clambered.
I sipped my coffee.
I thought I was having a bad trip,
hallucinating, on some kind of mind bend.
What was in this coffee anyway?

He continued mouthing silently.
I began to imagine him ripping me open and wearing my
young skin like a suit.
I looked down.
I could not keep his stare.

Was he cursing or was it a plea?
I knew I was not strong enough for this,
before the light changed,
I ran across the street to the other side.
He did not follow me and when I looked back he had left.

# The Boiling Shrimp

We are susceptible to the boiling shrimp of the glass eye.
The bubbling curd that towers and feeds
the ancient goddesses fertile and naked.
A short garrison man appears.
His limbs sparkle and shade,
enticing me to sit.

Abandoning my shoes across
the dirty wall of time,
in its Victorian hats, gloves and dresses
bow to an admiral off a ship that drowned years ago.

'I anticipate a change,' he said.
But the lips pursed,
and there is a muttering sound in the darkness around him.

Deeper I squint,
and molt the shell around me to see.
Where are the sacred woods? I asked,
where is the ancient fair?

The little angry man duplicated,
and the hourglass was turned over for me another time.

## Shadows Allure

Glistening windows, listless doors
the man rolls his last with a painful grip.
Finding his route
through the saki spilled streets.
Voices unknown
in a language unspoken.
Children buying swords.
Red and white lanterns drape above
without light,
charming the white moccasin girl
who walks with an unknown limp.

"Do you sell cigarettes here?"
said the man in a blue missoni suit.
He notices a rat outside
struggling to find warmth in the wedge of the door.

A bucket had been placed over it.
"My brain is not working well", the clerk said,
collecting his change.

Head up, don't let the pavement get you down
your rearview mirror is out of line
but the garage door is shut,
and the wind howls in time.

Children stare at the shadow over them.
Bonded in ribbons for an eternity.
His head wrap streaks into oblivion
illuminated from below by an overturned lamp.

## Chelsea Hotel
## Vandalism and other changes removed

The soul is an overturned vase.
What fills it is every piece of dust and trash,
from the deceased and lost.

Whatever good may bring of it are the quenched lips of the
squatting drunk, hoping it is not fully devoured.

Bent chariots roll aside the sideshow heir,
the festering obscurity demands relevance as it is stored aside,
unsure of the dream.

Edit:
the last room is carpeted,
sitting atop a three footed chair.
Insects beat
the primordial self
raising secrets out of pain.

Listen. Listen!
The candles burn
and the spirit
expells a green pool
of unseen delusions
felt within.

The marauding residents
Morrison, Nico, Dylan.
There are other rooms upstairs
for the forgotten ones.
Housed inside the red bricked limo
frantically uncoiling energy
and cutting off their tails.

One spoke with shivers:
"I've been waiting here
for eleven years.
I am simply asking
for a patch of yours."

Drowning out the words,
was a whisper down the hall.

"I am no more a junkie
than the other man."

Have you awoken yet?
Knowing you have lost the key?

# Jumping the Curb

In a silver toad-shaped car
he sped away listening to that Mexican polka beat.
Always thinking of what to do next,
while the padlock separates.

White sliding doors,
muttering foretold.
That they transferred a vein
from her leg into her heart.

A spider sits across the cornea
where words and lyric
no longer sell.

I jumped the curb
to free myself.

I jumped the curb
to see.

I'm on my way,
the driver finds my approach
and veers toward me.

It is my choice
to take it or race behind.

The splintering nest sings
against the dead laying giants.

# Comforting a Dying Mantis

Tears of life
puddle the ground
as we see our own reflection.

Mud honeys our ancestors
our home beneath the ground
below the bent oak and pine.

The titled tiles
lift your vitality
one day I will be.

The fading fire
splits and cracks
a mourning dove sings.

We lose our charms
hanging in trees
one day I will be.

Capered and gone
the branches drop
sadness consumes over me.

The playful gate
your profane fate
holding you in my arms.

Death the old child
splashes again
under his unsoiled boots.

Rippled and leaves
written treatise
letters of own time.

You are gone
away from me
one day I will be
with you again.

## Buzz and Flutter

You that carries life,
bring to me into your thoughts.
Flutter and buzz I say,
absent of this trivial walk.
Sting to me with a striking blow,
and paralyze my every sense.
I wish to breath your words again,
so that I may see and re-begin.
Strike, strike, little blue bee,
and feed me with your soul.
My eyes have swelled,
and I have no more,
encompassed within your shell.
Jet, dodge, and flee I seek,
there's a sight of violent weeds.
Consume, consume, oh giant white bug.
Is the taste not sour or rough?
Dig underneath,
and bury me aside,
In a wet parch of dirt.
Circle, circle, and devour,
I have found this place of worth.
But as the pain begins to hour,
I see myself again,
under a new leaf,
bound by sand,
No longer the same way in.

# The Persistent Fly

The world is not grafted upon the lids of the biosphere,
but the touch of humanity where all is consumed.
Discarded shells grind together to make the sand.
Bleeding oil and the siren screams.
The walrus watches carefully
with oversized beige glasses,
picking it's teeth.
Flies circle and feed off its sweat.
I can see the blue veins in the bright neon lights.
The mighty movers.
The sixties handsome eating LSD.
Spreading arms out like swarming plagues.
Freedom. 1-2-3.
Freedom.
For you and me.
Branded.
Freedom - now meaningless.

The walrus plays dress up for those underneath
as the fly remains persistent,
waiting to taste its reward or die trying.

## **Pendulum**

The pendulum swings
Slightly more
Slightly less.
Two of the same faces
with a different name.
Forced to mine
Your mind
does it allow
access to the inner stress.

Pounding out history
On a steel grid
Massively confused
Paranoia.

Children dancing
on a skeleton in marble.
And she
foresees
over glass
buttons latched
pulling her braided dress back.

A Capsule in motion
Honeycombed
A Tree house grave.
I don't want to leave this town
So the lariat swings free.
Blinking lights of the city night
Juggling waste in thin air
Stay with me
Observer
Just the same if you care.

**The Lorin Morgan-Richards Collection**

Simon Snootle and OTHER small stories

A Boy Born from Mold and Other Delectable Morsels

Dark Letter Days: Collected Works

Me'ma and the Great Mountain

A Dredged Summons and Other Misplaced Bills

The Night Speaks to Me

The Goodbye Family Album

**www.lorinrichards.com**

**www.aravenabovepress.com**

Lorin Morgan-Richards (b.1975) is an author, poet and illustrator, known mostly for his children's books. Richards is also the publisher of Celtic Family Magazine and is active in the Welsh American community.

"Lorin Morgan-Richards charts the paths of weird clouds that pass far overhead and then maps the changes that their rain makes on the lives of people living below."-Dark in the Dark Magazine

"Lorin Morgan-Richards has a unique tone and style all his own, and the stories are told in a fashion that pulls the casual reader in with wonderful fancy and the magical quality of good story telling. The high quality illustrations are rendered in sharp crisp lines and add to the wonderment instilled by these fanciful tales."-Macabre Cadaver Magazine

www.ingramcontent.com/pod-product-compliance
Lightning Source LLC
Chambersburg PA
CBHW040331300426
44113CB00020B/2719